Just Beachy
Bestest Buddies at the Beach

Written by William Wahr

Illustrated by Mary Wahr

Copyright: Mary Wahr
ISBN: 9781735703633

Hey there. My name is Roland.
I am a singin', cunnin', runnin',
rollie pollie poodle.
I love to bark and play all day.
ALL day!

This here is my bestest buddy, Chuckin' Chicken.
Hey, Chuckin', say hello.
HARUMMMPH!
That is no way to say hey.
You are such a chicken in the mud.

Today we're going to do one of my favorite things in the whole wide world.
Do you know what that is Chuckin'?
Stay home and roost?
No waayyy! We're going to the beach.

It sure is a beautiful day, isn't it Chuckin'?
Don't you just LOVE the wind and the sand
and the water and the sun?
Not really, dog.
LET ME OUT OF YOUR MOUTH!

Chuckin' Chicken, stop running away and have some fun.
AAAAHHHHH!

Look out Chuckin', I'm gonna get you!!
AAAAHHHH!!

AH HA, I finally got you.
Now let's play dig the Chuckin' Chicken.
UUUUHHH, you're standing on my head.

Chuckin' Chicken where did you go?
Chuckin' whispers, I'm hiding in plain sight, you silly poodle. Now, if I just stay still, maybe I can escape this jolly jerk!

Ptooey, ptooey. I sure do hate all the sand at the beach.
There you are, Chuckin', I guess now that we played dig, it's time to play..mm...m..shake!
No, Roland anything but that!!

Isn't this great Chuckin'? We play shake
and get all the sand off of you.
You know what, Roland?
This is actually kind of fun.
If you think this is fun, just wait!

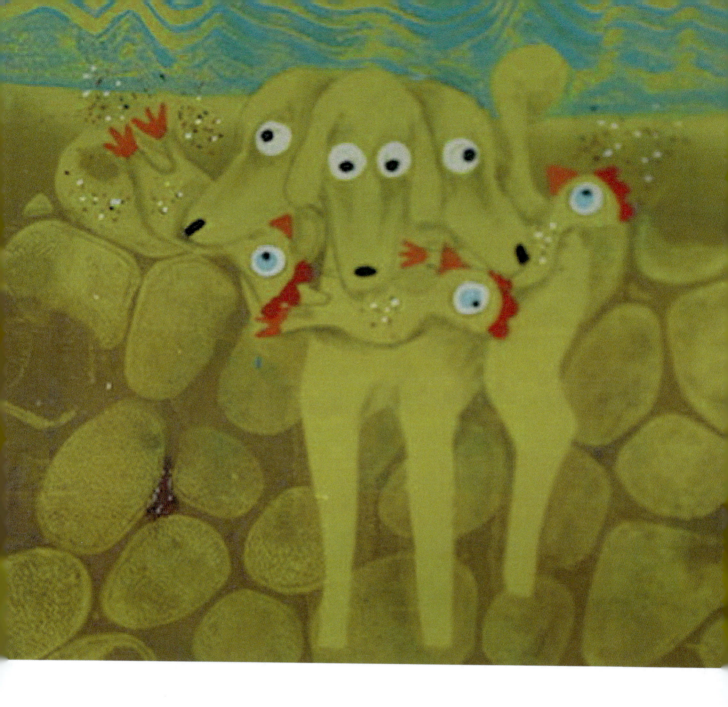

Maximum speed, maximum fun!

BBBWWWWWWAAAAA

Now a little swim and you'll feel brand new.
I'm pretty sure I'm going to spill my gizzards.
Boy, that sounds like a fun thing to do When you're done, let's play flying chicken.
OH NO!!

Well, this is going to happen whether I like it or not, so.....let's fly.
YOKOHAMA!

Look at you, my tryin', flyin, death defyin' often sighin' buddy. You are getting some air.
You will never catch me,
you peppy, pesky poodle.

I got you Chuckin'.
I don't think so, poodle!

No way, you really got up there.
Too high for you, Roland?
Give me another chance, Chuckin'.

Whoa, you got me doin' circles, Chuckin'.

Now this is turning into a fun day at the beach!

Gotcha, Chuckin'. Geez, I had no idea how good you were at flying around.

Roland, that turned out to be a lot of fun. I am glad I wasn't at home cooped up all day.

What a day! Are you ready to go home, pal?
Almost, but now I'm lying in the sand.
How about we play another game of shake?

Interesting Facts

Chuckin' uses the word Yokohama when he takes flight. He uses it in honor of the Japanese chicken that was exported to Europe in 1864. These chickens were shipped from the port of Yokohama. Hence their name. Today they are mostly show chickens because of their long beautiful tails.

Can chickens swim?
You bet they can. They may not have webbed feet like a duck, but they can swim.

Made in the USA
Middletown, DE
18 November 2020